The Baby Made Me Buy It!

A Treasury of Babies
Who Sold Yesterday's Products

Written and designed by

ALICE L. MUNCASTER, ELLEN SAWYER,
and KEN KAPSON

Photography by Peter Basdeka

CROWN PUBLISHERS, INC.
NEW YORK

To our parents
(for obvious reasons)

Cover art courtesy of The William Carter Company

Published by Crown Publishers, Inc., 201 East 50th Street, New York, New York 10022. Member of The Crown Publishing Group.

CROWN is a trademark of Crown Publishers, Inc.

Manufactured in Hong Kong

Library of Congress Cataloging-in-Publication Data

Muncaster, Alice L.
The baby made me buy it! : a treasury of babies who sold
yesterday's products / written and designed by Alice L. Muncaster,
Ellen Sawyer, and Ken Kapson : photographs by Peter Basdeka.
1. Children in advertising—United States—History.
2. Advertising—Psychological aspects.   I. Sawyer, Ellen.
II. Kapson, Ken.   III. Title.
HF5813.U6M76   1991

659.1—dc20   90-19800
                                                                          CIP

ISBN 0-517-58206-6
10 9 8 7 6 5 4 3 2 1
First Edition

Introduction

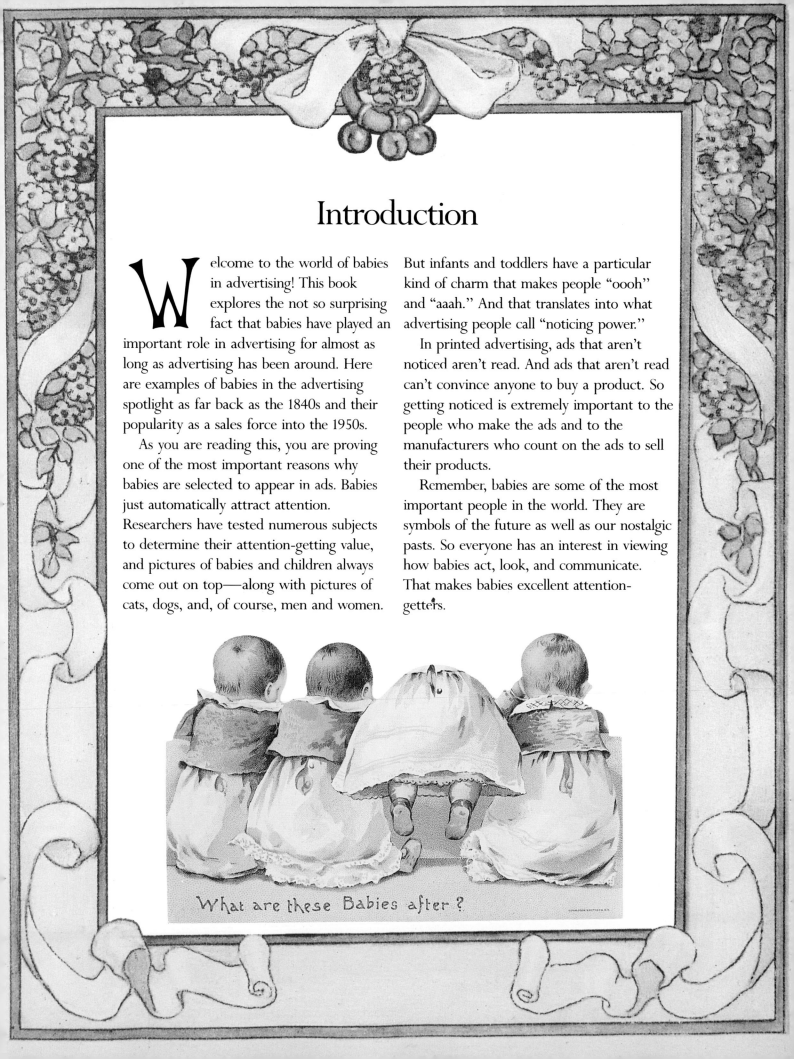

Welcome to the world of babies in advertising! This book explores the not so surprising fact that babies have played an important role in advertising for almost as long as advertising has been around. Here are examples of babies in the advertising spotlight as far back as the 1840s and their popularity as a sales force into the 1950s.

As you are reading this, you are proving one of the most important reasons why babies are selected to appear in ads. Babies just automatically attract attention. Researchers have tested numerous subjects to determine their attention-getting value, and pictures of babies and children always come out on top—along with pictures of cats, dogs, and, of course, men and women.

But infants and toddlers have a particular kind of charm that makes people "oooh" and "aaah." And that translates into what advertising people call "noticing power."

In printed advertising, ads that aren't noticed aren't read. And ads that aren't read can't convince anyone to buy a product. So getting noticed is extremely important to the people who make the ads and to the manufacturers who count on the ads to sell their products.

Remember, babies are some of the most important people in the world. They are symbols of the future as well as our nostalgic pasts. So everyone has an interest in viewing how babies act, look, and communicate. That makes babies excellent attention-getters.

What are these Babies after?

As we selected images for this book, we limited our search to advertising of the past. After all, anyone can turn on the television today and see babies in commercials. We wanted to introduce you to the beautiful images created during the Victorian Era of the late 1800s, and show you how twentieth-century advertising looked before radio and television became the dominant sales media.

Through our search, we found that babies were often the stars of ads for "baby products"—such as infant formula and talcum powder. But many other kinds of products also had help from the little ones, and quite a few products actually had *baby* as part of their brand names—Baby Rice Pop Corn, Baby Bunting Candy, Cry Baby Grapes, and Baby Mine Powder, for example.

Perhaps the most interesting part of our research was investigating the origins of those baby-named products. Our hope was to find out if they were named for real babies—and, if so, to determine who they were and what became of them. We were pleased to find the answers to some of our questions but, sadly, we found that the history surrounding many products has been lost.

As you turn the pages, you'll find that the advertising follows some general themes. Babies are shown, for the most part, in idyllic cradle scenes, being held by their mothers, or playing with other children. There are a number of scenes showing babies with pets, such as cats and dogs, and, occasionally, a father is shown with a child. In a few cases, a nanny can be seen taking care of the baby. This is not surprising since advertising generally reflects societal trends, and women were generally considered responsible for child care and housekeeping during the time this advertising was created. Men, on the other hand, related somewhat

Infant formula products were often promoted on advertising cards such as this beautiful two-sided die-cut from the late 1800s. Wells Richardson & Company's advertising used endorsements from doctors to point out the need for good nourishment in the first eighteen months of a baby's life. Many ads from this period show babies with pets, since cats and dogs are natural family companions.

America's early baby powder business was highly competitive. When this ad appeared in *The Theatre* magazine in 1909, the Gerhard Mennen Co. was one of the leading manufacturers but had to defend its reputation against underpriced imitations. Mennen revolutionized the baby powder industry with a soothing medicated formula and a shaker-top box. Until then, most powders were sold in boxes that, when opened, were easily contaminated. Mennen's Borated Talcum Toilet Powder was introduced in 1889 with a rose fragrance. Free samples of a new violet-scented version were offered in this ad.

differently to babies—as you'll see in the way advertising for some of the more masculine products was created.

You'll also notice that this early advertising does not feature people from a variety of ethnic backgrounds. In fact, we found that blacks, Native Americans, Orientals, and Hispanics were largely ignored. This was because the advertisers tried to appeal to the consumer they thought was most likely to buy their product—presumably whites of European descent.

"Fantasy babies" were fashionable before the turn of the century. Cupids and cherubs delighted the romantic Victorians in books, prints, and, of course, advertising. In the early 1900s, Kewpies were the rage, just as today cartoon characters are widely used in advertising and merchandising.

You may also notice that there are early ads in this book for products that are still in existence. We found it interesting that so many of today's successful companies had their roots in the late 1800s and early 1900s. We also found that advertising from these early times was not so different from today's advertising, after all.

The late 1800s is considered to be the beginning of advertising's modern era. Newly invented high-speed printing presses made colorful advertising widely available for the first time in America. Printing companies sold manufacturers and even store owners on the idea of promoting their products via this new medium. Magazines gradually included color covers and advertising. But the most important new advertising source was the advertising "trade card"—small cards that were imprinted with a beautiful illustration on the front and advertising on the back. People had never seen such colorful images and such a great variety of art, so these cards were saved and, fortunately for today's collectors, placed in scrapbooks.

Besides examples of these advertising cards, you'll find babies on a variety of promotional premiums—useful everyday items that carry a printed

Mothers holding their babies are familiar pictures in both advertising and publishing. The advertising card at the left is from the late 1800s, and promoted a patent medicine that was popular at the time. The card was produced before the Food and Drug Act of 1906 required disclosure of the contents of such medicines—Mrs. Winslow's contained a liberal dose of opium! *The Delineator* magazine began in 1873 and grew to become one of the largest and most popular women's fashion magazines. It was started by the Butterick family, and their sewing patterns were originally offered as premiums with a subscription order. The poignant cover at the right appeared at the end of World War I. *The Delineator* was combined with a Hearst magazine—*Pictorial Review*—in 1937.

THE DELINEATOR

— July 1919 —

HOME TOMORROW

MABEL POTTER DAGGETT'S "THE TOWN OF THE GOLDEN BOOK."
STORIES BY GRACE SARTWELL MASON, DEMETRA VAKA, JAMES
F. DWYER, PHYLLIS BOTTOME. ❧ LATEST MIDSUMMER FASHIONS

TWENTY CENTS
THE COPY

THE BUTTERICK PUBLISHING COMPANY, NEW YORK

$2.00 A YEAR
$2.50 IN CANADA

The Edison Phonograph Company of West Orange, New Jersey, appealed to the intellect with quotes from Shakespeare and to every mother's heart with the baby faces featured on this advertising card from about 1908. Thomas Edison introduced his first cylinder phonograph in 1877. During his lifetime, Edison received 1,093 patents, over half of which were developed at his West Orange laboratory. Among his inventions were motion-picture equipment, storage batteries, a fluoroscope used in the first X-ray operation in the United States, and, of course, the light bulb. The phonograph shown above is the "Home" Model B, introduced in 1906.

advertising message, such as calendars, hand-held fans, ink blotters, and pocket mirrors. And you'll see tiny boys and girls on everything from product packages and labels to magazine ads, magazine covers, sheet music, in-store displays, and posters.

Can a baby make you buy a product? Only you can answer that question. But thousands of people did buy the products babies endorsed, making these "salesbabies" very successful indeed. In fact, their selling power is as strong today as it was when the advertising was produced. We hope you enjoy meeting them!

Parents love to keep records of babies' measurements and "firsts"—such as first step, first tooth, and first word. Throughout the years, companies have appealed to this interest by creating "baby books" that were given free to new parents. Beautifully illustrated pages provided space for recording baby's activities, and a few pages of product advertising were also included for easy reference. "Baby's Red Letter Days" was produced in 1900 by Just's Food Co. of Syracuse, New York. Just's Food was a milk substitute for babies and invalids. "Baby's Record" was produced by The Knapp Co., Inc., in 1913 and was offered by the First National Bank of Greenville, South Carolina. The Metropolitan Life Insurance Company produced "Baby's Book" from 1923 to 1939. And the John Carle & Sons Co. of New York produced "Our Baby's Own Book" in 1918. Through poetry, the book promoted Imperial Granum, an unsweetened cereal product made for infants, convalescents, and the elderly.

Fresh milk was not always easily available in the 1800s, and storage of milk to prevent spoilage was difficult. But Gail Borden discovered a process that preserved milk by condensation in a vacuum, so that milk could be canned for easy storage at home or while traveling. This breakthrough gave mothers the opportunity to provide babies a wholesome milk product almost anywhere. Borden started his company in 1857 and it became the New York Condensed Milk Co. in 1858. The advertising card above (enlarged) is from the late 1800s. The poster at the right, which measures 21¼″ high × 14″ wide, is dated 1887. It was probably displayed in general stores that sold Borden products. Directions printed on the back of both pieces explain how to mix condensed milk with water to create an infant's formula. Although Gail Borden died in 1874, his company lives on as Borden, Inc., a diversified corporation that, in addition to producing milk products, is a leading producer of food products, such as pasta, salty snacks, and sauces, and such nonfood products as wall coverings.

This beautiful die-cut advertising piece was found in a Victorian scrapbook. The image of the baby and puppy in the center was also produced as an advertising card that could be imprinted with the names of various Borden companies, including, in 1891, The Illinois Condensing Co. of Chicago. That company was established in 1862 to manufacture Borden's Condensed Milk in the Midwest, and existed until 1895. This larger advertising keepsake, which was originally attached to a handle to create a fan, was given away by the New York Condensed Milk Co., the parent Borden company. It shows the addition of a bottled milk product. Distribution of Borden's fluid milk in bottles began in 1885.

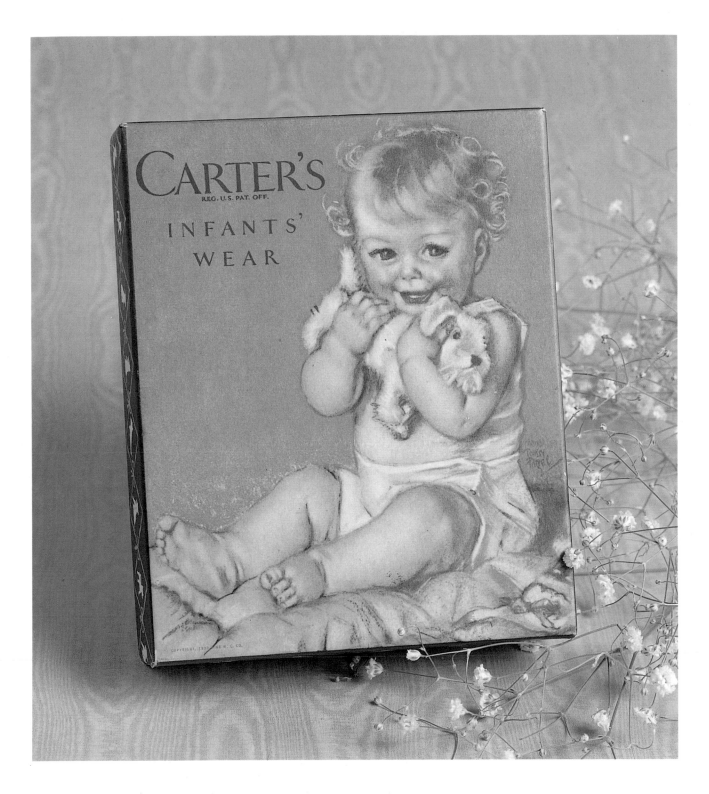

Carter's Infants' Wear was packaged in this beautiful box illustrated by Maud Tousey Fangel during the 1930s. William B. Carter was a knitting machine operator who came to America from England in 1856. He started The William Carter Company in 1865, primarily making knitted cardigan jackets in the kitchen of his Needham Heights, Massachusetts, home. When a large quantity of yarn was destroyed by moths, Carter ingeniously used the remainder to make tiny mittens for children. They were so popular that the company added children's apparel to its permanent line of goods. Today, Carter's is one of America's best-known brands. The company manufactures over 40 million garments a year in its full line of layette wear for newborns, and children's underwear, sleepwear, and playwear.

Children are naturally attracted to babies, as demonstrated by the cover illustration at right from *The Modern Priscilla* magazine. This publication was one of the most popular women's magazines in the early years of this century. Its pages were filled with information that was useful to homemakers, even including dress patterns and china-painting directions. It was published from 1887 to 1930.

Victorian advertising cards give us a look at the fashions and lifestyles of an earlier time. Because color printing was still new to America before 1900, people actively collected and saved these colorful cards. Companies and stores usually created a variety of giveaway cards showing various scenes. So even though these two examples show a more affluent way of life than most people enjoyed, they were not necessarily directed only to wealthy customers. Kerr & Company produced cotton sewing thread in Newark, New Jersey, around the turn of the century and in New York until operations ceased in 1946. The Massachusetts Shoe House card promoted a local retail merchant in Upstate New York.

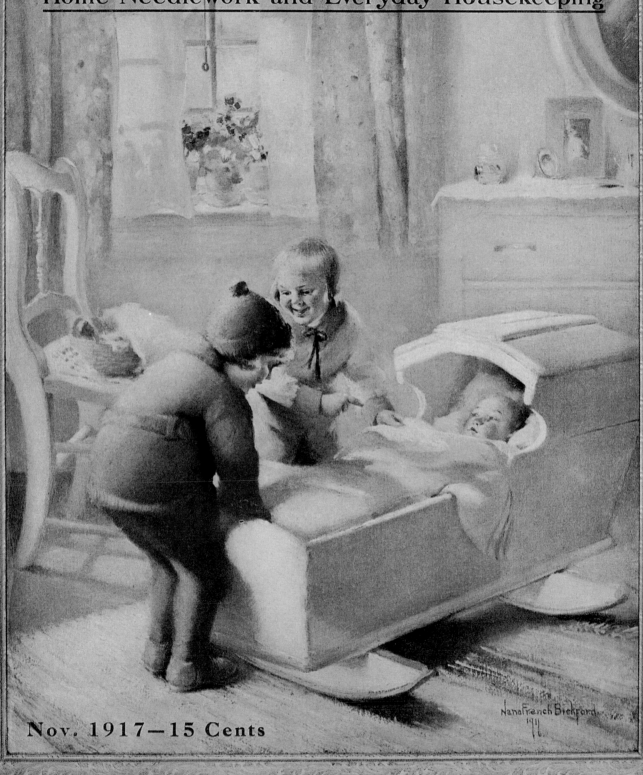

THE Modern Priscilla

Home Needlework and Everyday Housekeeping

Nov. 1917—15 Cents

To keep babies' skin soft and dry, mothers know talcum powder is a must. But in the late 1800s, many powders for babies contained a mixture of cornstarch and chalk, which often resulted in caking and skin irritation. In those olden days, pharmacists experimented with creating proprietary medicines—and it was Gerhard Mennen who discovered a way to improve upon the traditional baby powder formulas. Mennen emigrated from Germany to America when he was fifteen years old, and received his pharmacy degree just four years later. He experimented with carbolated talcum, a mineral that was not affected by heat or moisture. Then he added boracic acid for its antiseptic properties, and oil of roses for a delicate scent. This "Borated Talcum" Toilet Powder was introduced in his Newark, New Jersey, pharmacy in July 1889. The advertising card at the right was used before 1900 to promote the brand. The beautifully lithographed two-sided tin store fixture (*below*) dramatically displayed the product just after the turn of the century. The magazine advertisement (*far right*) appeared in *The Theatre* magazine in 1905. Babies were prominently used in Mennen's advertising, and "Baby's Best Friend" was a slogan used in 1908. Today, Mennen's Baby Magic Baby Powder is an updated version of the original product.

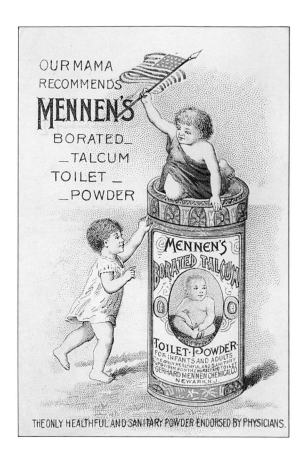

16

LIKE A COOLING BREEZE

is the gentle touch of Mennen's. Just as a cooling breeze on a hot Summer day is welcomed for the relief it brings, so will your parched skin, irritated by **Prickly Heat**, **Chafing** or **Sunburn**, welcome

MENNEN'S BORATED TALCUM TOILET POWDER

for its cooling, soothing and healing effect. After bathing, after shaving and for infants it is refreshing and delightful.

Not on our package, but on our Powder, we have built our national reputation. See that you get the original. Avoid ordinary powders, highly scented with cheap perfume and put up in ornamental packages. The price of great success is a host of imitators. Don't be misled by the unscrupulous dealer, who says: "Just as good."

SOLD EVERYWHERE OR BY MAIL, 25 CENTS.   SAMPLE FREE.   GERHARD MENNEN CO., 1 ORANGE ST., NEWARK, N. J.

TRY MENNEN'S VIOLET TALCUM

THE THEATRE 1905   F. SHARLES, LITHO., N. Y.

The baby on the Baby Rice Pop Corn package was actually the son of the company's founder. Matthias Voelker's son John smiled out from the label on the can above and from the updated store window decal at the left. Matt Voelker was one of Waterloo, Wisconsin's leading businessmen. He began his career by operating a feed store, and convinced local—and then regional—farmers to plant seeds for the corn he thought produced the most tender popped corn. He called it Baby Rice, and it is said to be the first hulless popcorn. Railroad carloads of Baby Rice were soon being shipped all over America and to foreign countries as well. The Baby Rice image appeared on bags used by popcorn vendors who sold the brand and in national advertising. The company made several other popcorn brands, yet Baby Rice was the best seller through 1941, when the company ceased operations. If you have the opportunity to see the 1933 movie *State Fair*, look for the bag of Baby Rice Pop Corn in the hands of Will Rogers.

Many advertisements for Mentholatum antiseptic cream have pictured babies and children, since children often gets cuts and bruises as a result of their active and play-filled lifestyles. "The Little Nurse" theme was personified for many years by a winsome little girl dressed as a nurse. The Mentholatum Company was started in 1889 by Albert A. Hyde, a Wichita, Kansas, druggist. He first called the company the Yucca Co., since the primary product was soap made from the yucca cactus plant. Another product was a medicated menthol ointment, and in 1894 it was introduced as Mentholatum. The Buffalo, New York, factory was opened in 1903 and the company officially became The Mentholatum Company in 1906, helping to date when the ink blotter shown above was made. Today, the company produces over-the-counter health-care products including, of course, Mentholatum.

The babies on this advertising card for Dr. J. C. Ayer & Co. are shown packing Ayer's Cathartic Pills into round wooden boxes for retail sale. During the late 1800s, when advertising cards like this were given away to customers at general stores, babies were often depicted as elves, cherubs, or angels, performing adult tasks. Ayer's Cathartic Pills were first produced in 1850. Although the formula changed over the next few decades, an important ingredient was always castor oil, leaving no doubt as to its laxative effects. The pills were advertised as a blood purifier and offered relief from dyspepsia, described as a disease of the muscular fibrous coating of the stomach. Dr. Ayer died in 1878, but his company went on to become one of the most prominent patent-medicine companies of the nineteenth century. Ayer's Pills are no longer made.

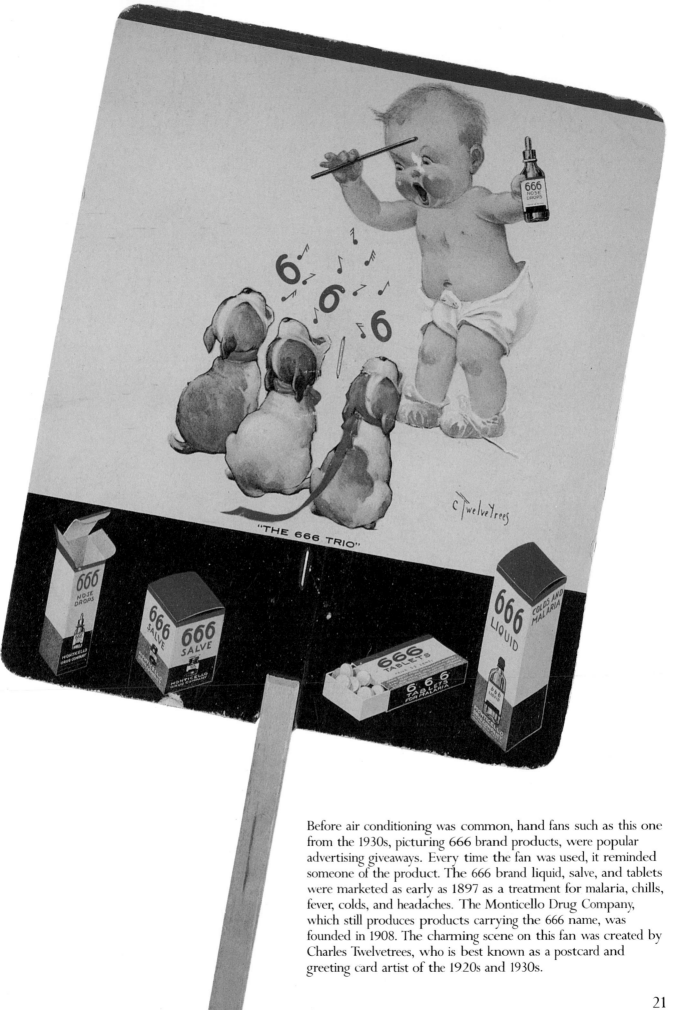

"THE 666 TRIO"

Before air conditioning was common, hand fans such as this one from the 1930s, picturing 666 brand products, were popular advertising giveaways. Every time the fan was used, it reminded someone of the product. The 666 brand liquid, salve, and tablets were marketed as early as 1897 as a treatment for malaria, chills, fever, colds, and headaches. The Monticello Drug Company, which still produces products carrying the 666 name, was founded in 1908. The charming scene on this fan was created by Charles Twelvetrees, who is best known as a postcard and greeting card artist of the 1920s and 1930s.

ROSE petals are not softer, violets not sweeter, than the baby refreshed by the silken touch of Williams' Baby Talc.

Fine and smooth, delicately fragrant, it soothes the most tender places and leads on to quiet sleep.

There are also Williams' Talcs for all the older members of the family—for every use—after the bath, at the dressing table, after exercise and exposure.

The can is larger and gives a more generous quantity—quality considered—than any other powder.

The convenient hinged cover prevents waste, and keeps the fragrance until the last is used.

Williams' Talc Powder

Shaving Soaps, Talc Powders, Toilet Soaps, Toilet Waters, Dental Cream and Powder, Cold Cream and Toilet Luxuries.

What is your favorite perfume in talc? Williams' has six—Violet, Carnation, English Lilac, Matinée, Rose and Baby Talc. Send 4c. in stamps for sample of any of these to

THE J. B. WILLIAMS COMPANY
Glastonbury, Conn.

Mothers in the 'teens and the 1920s could choose from many brands of baby talcum powders. To shoppers in those days, it must have seemed that each new talc container introduced was more beautiful than the preceding one. The J. B. Williams Company of Glastonbury, Connecticut, offered talc tins featuring charming baby faces during this era. The tin shown in the 1919 magazine advertisement at the left was followed in 1920 by the one shown above. This particularly colorful tin also had the "flip-top" feature described in the magazine ad.

James B. Williams started his company in 1840. At first, he made only shaving soap, but he almost immediately branched out to make ink and shoe blacking. By the turn of the century, the diversified company was making toilet soaps and Ivorine cleanser, a disinfectant soap used for household washing and laundry. Williams's shaving soap can still be found at pharmacies today, but the baby talc is no longer made.

The United Drug Company, founded in Boston in 1903, offered the delicately designed tin at the right, above, in the 1920s. Many of the company's products used the "Rexall" brand, a name that means "king of all." It is still possible to find Rexall brand products, but the chain of drugstores that once used the Rexall name no longer exists.

Pets guarding baby was the theme of this late nineteenth-century advertising card for the Michigan Stove Company. It promoted both kitchen ranges and household stoves. Babies need warmth and even temperatures in cold weather, so many stove manufacturers of the time cited "even heating" as the benefit of heating a home with their brand of stove instead of a competitor's. The Michigan Stove Company began in 1873, consolidated with the Detroit Stove Works in 1925, and was purchased by the Welbilt Corporation in 1955. The Garland brand name is still in use today.

Hires® Root Beer is a familiar brand to shoppers today, just as it has been for generations. The Charles E. Hires Company has been producing the popular drink since the founder, Charles Hires, first offered it to consumers in the 1870s. His famous recipe was first packaged like tea in a cheesecloth bag. Then he formulated a dry water-soluble extract, but sugar and yeast had to be added before drinking it. In 1880, Hires marketed a liquid concentrate, and ready-to-drink bottles were available by 1893. The company advertised extensively, using advertising cards like the one shown at left before the turn of the century. Another Hires card can be seen pictured beside the glass on the table. That image of a small child, and the baby shown here, are two of Hires's most recognizable advertisements. Hires Root Beer is still quenching thirst today.

Mothers know they need a gentle soap to wash delicate baby skin. And for shoppers, baby soap is easily recognizable if a baby is pictured on the package. These two soaps, however, were not generally sold in stores, but through distributors or agents. Dr. Blumer's Baby Toilet Soap was offered by the Lincoln Chemical Works, probably in the 1930s. The company dates back to 1886, when it was founded by Dr. Robert Blumer, who had his factory in his home in Chicago. The company no longer exists. California Baby Soap was made by the California Perfume Company of New York in the late 1800s and early 1900s. The company was founded in 1886 by David McConnell, a door-to-door book salesman, who discovered that women were more likely to invite him into their homes if he first gave them a small present such as perfume. When he found that the perfume was in more demand than books, he decided to go into the perfume-manufacturing business instead. He employed a general agent—Mrs. P. F. E. Albee—to travel through New England offering his products, and she in turn recruited women in each community to sell the perfumes to friends. Today, this company is a thriving international corporation known as Avon Products, Inc.

Always ready for Kellogg's Toasted Corn Flakes

Children tire of *drinking* milk; but the wise mother smiles and pours the milk plentifully into a big bowlful of Kellogg's. Children are always ready for Kellogg's—the original Toasted Corn Flakes, *thin, crisp and appetizing.*

KRUMBLES is Kellogg's *all-wheat* food. Every single tiny shred is thoroughly toasted.

W. K. Kellogg

Kellogg's
TOASTED
CORN
FLAKES
THE ORIGINAL HAS THIS SIGNATURE
W. K. Kellogg
KELLOGG TOASTED CORN FLAKE CO.
BATTLE CREEK, MICH.
NET WEIGHT 10 OUNCES

WAXTITE

W. K. Kellogg and his brother developed Kellogg's Toasted Corn Flakes in 1898. These early examples of the company's advertising show how from the early years of this century, the company has used beautiful and realistic art to promote its products. The die-cut two-sided sign at the right measures 13½″ × 19½″ and was used in stores beginning in 1910. It is lithographed tin, manufactured by the American Art Works Co. of Cochocton, Ohio, the premier U.S. advertising lithography source of that time. The full-page magazine advertisement above is from 1917. This charming child was drawn by J. C. Leyendecker, one of the nation's most popular commercial illustrators, from about 1900 until his death in 1951. Starting the day with Kellogg's Corn Flakes is a breakfast tradition millions of people still enjoy.

An illustration with a holiday flavor made this magazine ad from December 1920 particularly appropriate for the season. Artist Torre Bevans was an artist of the 1920s whose work was seen in advertising and on magazine covers of that time. Royal Baking Powder originated in 1873, and the Royal Baking Powder Company became part of the Nabisco family of products in 1981. This product is still sold in overseas markets.

Babies and children have played an important role over the years in advertising for Kellogg's cereal products. *Below left:* This full-page ad appeared in women's magazines in 1913. *Below right:* The scene on the cover of this 1917 leaflet showed that even babies would eagerly eat Kellogg's Toasted Wheat Biscuit. A coupon on the back offered a book of pictures and verses for children called "The Adventures of Willie Winters." This was an effective promotional tie-in because Kellogg's products were featured within the book. The leaflet described Kellogg's Toasted Wheat Biscuit as a type of breakfast biscuit that could be eaten buttered like toast or with milk as a cereal.

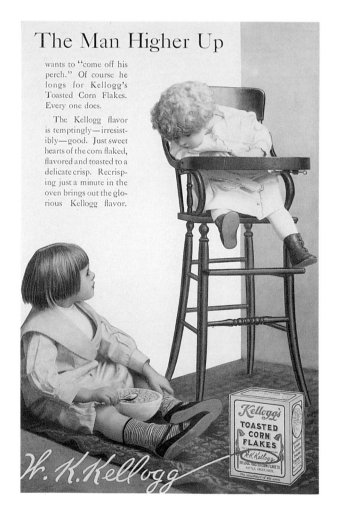

Dreaming of His Gingerbread Men

ROYAL
Baking Powder

Absolutely Pure

makes the best gingerbread, cookies, cakes
and biscuits.

Write today for the New Royal Cook Book
containing 400 delightful recipes. It's free.

ROYAL BAKING POWDER CO., 112 Fulton St., New York

A FAVORITE WITH THE LADIES.

Some of the most beautiful baby illustrations found on advertising cards of the Victorian era were created by two famous thread manufacturers, the George A. Clark Company and the J. & P. Coats company. During the late 1800s, women sewed and repaired their families' clothing, so a great number of cards featured babies or small children to appeal to female consumers. Both companies were family businesses that began in Paisley, Scotland—Clark in 1812 and Coats in 1820. By 1854, the Clarks had sent a family member to America to sell their thread, and U.S. manufacturing was soon set up. The Coats family followed in 1866. The two companies merged in 1952. The initials O.N.T. stood for "Our New Thread" on Clark's cards. Shown on the top left is an early card, probably from the 1880s, marked "George A. Clark, Sole Agent." The die-cut below, to which a small calendar pad was originally stapled, is dated 1895, and was issued by George A. Clark & Brother, Sole Agents. Both companies often pictured spools of thread being used in the illustrations of their advertising, sometimes showing them oversized, or as children's toys.

COLGATE'S TALC POWDER

COLGATE'S BABY TALC

This charming powder is exactly the same as our other Talc Powders, with the exception that the perfume is less pronounced, and for that reason may be preferred for the nursery
COLGATE & CO. — New York, U.S.A.
REG. U.S. PAT. OFF.

Five Points of Difference

All talcums are *not* alike—as so many people think. If habit alone governs your present choice, read these five reasons why Colgate's is safer and better for you and your children.

It contains just the right amount of boric acid, that mild and soothing, yet efficient antiseptic.

The perfumes not only add their delicate charm but actually increase the antiseptic value of the powder.

Colgate's is wonderfully fine and smooth—imparting a soothing and comfortable sensation to the skin.

Its absorbent, sanative qualities tend to neutralize the irritation of acid perspiration and to relieve chafing, sunburn, and windburn.

The convenient six-hole sifter top concentrates the flow of the powder and prevents waste.

Besides these reasons for preferring Colgate's to other talcums there is also the personal reason of a wider choice in perfume.

Sold everywhere—or a dainty trial box of any one sent for 4c in stamps

COLGATE & CO., Dept. J, 199 Fulton Street, New York
Canadian Address: Drummond Building, Montreal

Makers of Cashmere Bouquet Soap—luxurious, lasting, refined

110 years ago was founded the House of Colgate & Co.— to-day the world's largest makers of fine soaps and perfumes.

32

During the World War I era, shoppers looked for the winsome Colgate baby in advertising for the company's talc powder products. Both of these full-page magazine ads featuring the baby appeared in 1916, 110 years after William Colgate began his starch, soap, and candle business in New York. Cashmere Bouquet Talc complemented the soap of the same name, which was introduced in 1872. The Baby Talc tin displayed an unusual "infinity" design—repetition of the illustration of the baby holding the package, until it is too small to see. An example of this talc tin from around 1914–18 is shown below, along with a can of Comfort Powder. Comfort Powder was made by The Comfort Powder Company which was in business from 1891 to 1914 in Hartford, Connecticut. The clock is from about 1910–15 and provides some insight into the appeal of babies and cherubs in home decoration. Colgate merged with the fifty-six-year-old Palmolive-Peet Co. in 1928, and today the Colgate-Palmolive Company is one of the world's leading manufacturers of personal-care and household products. Cashmere Bouquet body powder is still produced.

A real baby inspired the owners of the Huggins Candy Company to feature the name
"Baby" in many of their early products. Louis Huggins, Sr., started the company about 1903
and baby-named candies began appearing after his first daughter, Bernice, was born. Sugar
sticks, caramel kisses, and chocolate and marshmallow confections, both handmade and
machine-dipped, were made at the four-story factory in Nashville, Tennessee. The company
was sold in 1932, but continued producing candy until around World War II.

The darling baby on the advertising fan shown at the right was drawn by Rose O'Neill, an
artist most famous for her drawings of Kewpies, fantasy creatures with tiny wings. Though
not a Kewpie, this baby was so cute it captured attention for the American Thermos Bottle
Company of New York in the 1920s or 1930s, just as it had in 1911, when it appeared on
the cover of a Sunday newspaper supplement (without the Thermos bottles). Information
about Thermos products was printed on the back of the fan, stating that a Thermos kept
liquids cold for three days and hot for twenty-four hours. An accompanying drawing of a
mother and baby was captioned with the fact that a Thermos could be indispensable in the
nursery as it kept milk cold, clean, germ-proof, and fly-proof. Thermos bottles, first
produced in 1907 when William B. Walker founded the company in Brooklyn, New York,
are still manufactured today.

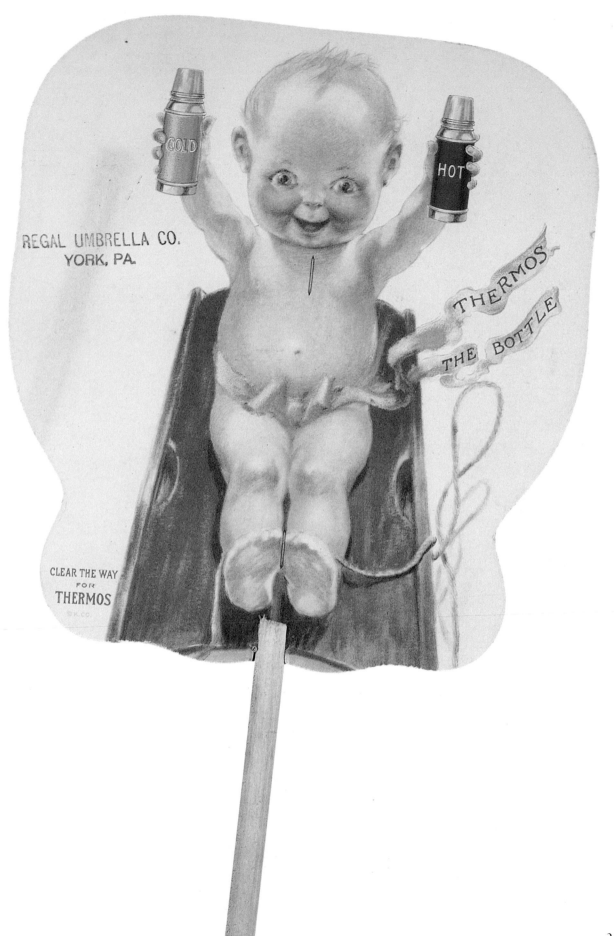

A baby fast asleep reminded readers of the 1925 magazine ad at the right that precious little lives can depend on reliable automobile tires. ("Balloon Cord" tires were inflatable tires. Some earlier tires were actually solid rubber.) Maud Tousey Fangel, the artist who drew the baby for this ad, was known for creating realistic baby likenesses directly from live models. Her beautiful pastels were familiar to magazine readers of the 1920s and 1930s, when much of her work appeared in advertisements and on magazine covers. When this ad appeared, The Fisk Tire Company had been using a sleepy little boy and the "Time to Re-Tire" slogan for about twenty years. They were designed in 1905 by Burr E. Giffen, who convinced the company's president to try them in advertising. They were so successful that they were trademarked in 1910. The Uniroyal Goodrich Tire Company still produces Fisk tires.

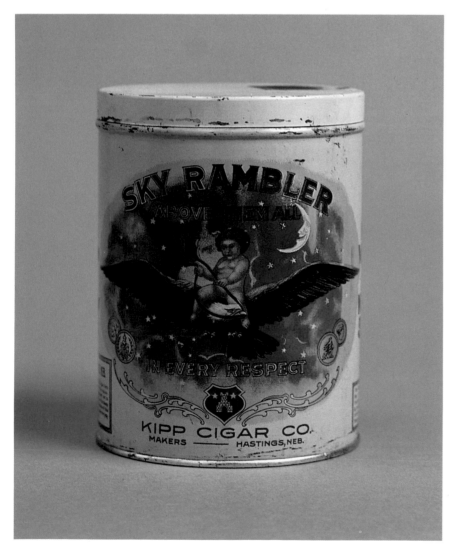

Early cigar companies were known for their intriguing brand names and beautiful label designs. Sky Rambler was a five-cent cigar made by the Kipp Cigar Company, at one time one of the largest cigar manufacturers in Nebraska. John Kipp started the company in 1909 and eventually employed one hundred cigar makers in his Hastings factory. At its peak, over 50,000 cigars were produced there daily, and Kipp cigars were sold in every state west of the Mississippi. Kipp also produced chewing tobacco beginning in 1922. As cigarettes grew in popularity in America after World War 1, demand for cigars decreased. The Kipp factory closed in 1930.

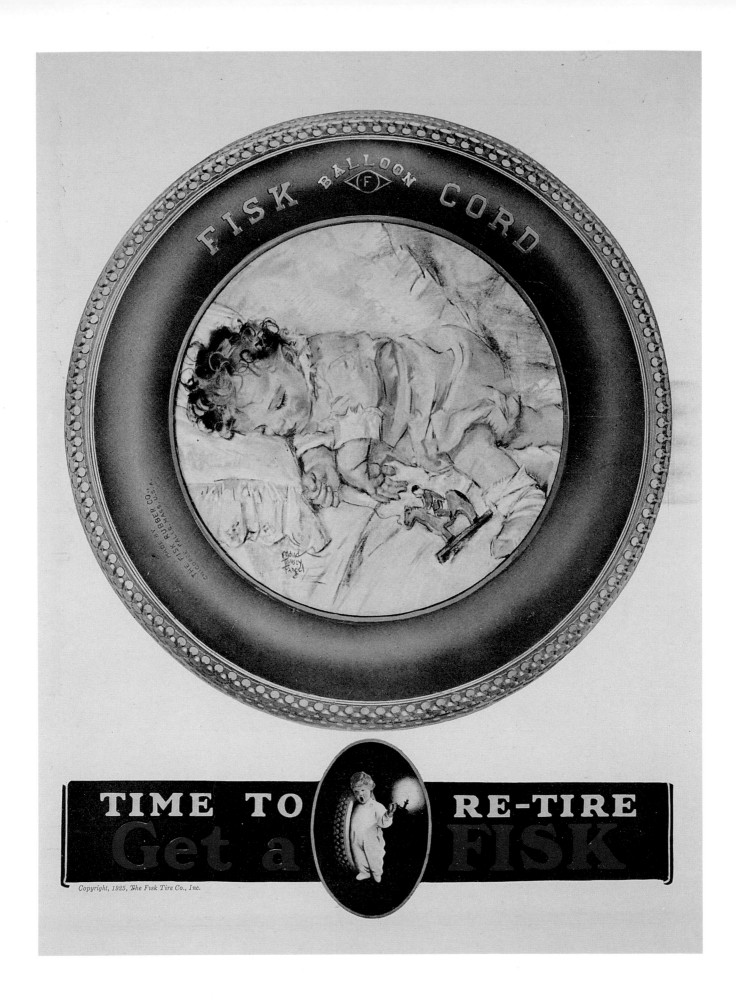

While many babies' likenesses were found on early product packages, this advertising envelope from 1903 for the Paris Medicine Company is quite unusual. Most envelopes of this type pictured a product or corporate logo. The company was founded by Edwin W. Grove, a druggist's clerk who eventually became a pharmaceutical manufacturing millionaire. He started the company at his home town of Paris, Tennessee, in 1889 and retained the name "Paris" when he moved the business to St. Louis, Missouri, two years later. Laxative Bromo Quinine tablets, an over-the-counter medication for treating colds, was the most successful of the company's products. In the early 1920s the Paris Medicine Company became Grove Laboratories, which was sold to the Bristol-Myers Company in the 1950s. LBQ tablets are no longer made.

Loving thoughts may come to mind at the mention of Cupid, so E. B. Millar & Co. of Chicago may have believed that such a pleasant association would help sell coffee of the same name. This type of charming coffee can would have been sold in general stores or groceries around the turn of the century. Earl B. Millar and George D. Rowan were importing teas in Chicago as early as 1876. Later, the company retained only Millar's name, and "Excelsior Mills" was used from around 1894 through the 1920s. Neither the company nor the product exist today.

Besides keeping cookies fresh, decorative biscuit tins make attractive keepsakes. This unusual tin container in the shape of a baby carriage is called "The Perambulator" and was produced only in 1930 for the British baking firm of Huntley & Palmers. An assortment of cookies was packed inside. The company dates back to 1822, when Joseph Huntley opened a biscuit bakery in Reading, England. His nephew, Thomas, assisted and later took over the business. Tin-lined boxes were first used by Huntley in the 1830s so that people could take a supply of the popular biscuits along when they traveled. George Palmers joined the company in 1841, bringing along new technology that allowed the business to expand into the mass production of quality biscuits. Today, Huntley & Palmers Foods, p.l.c., carries on the tradition of making fine cookies known the world over.

Whimsical floating babies amused subscribers to *People's Home Journal* in September 1926. This magazine was one of many "mail-order journals" for women published from the late 1800s until after the turn of the century. These publications were printed on thin, inexpensive paper and were filled with advertisements for products available by mail order. Even though such journals did carry fiction stories and household features, they were considered somewhat less legitimate than other women's periodicals of the time, because the heavy volume of advertising made them seem more like catalogs than magazines. *People's Home Journal* was published from 1886 to 1929.

The children and baby on this advertising card from the late 1800s demonstrated two uses for Highland brand evaporated milk from the Helvetia Milk Condensing Company. The product was advertised as a food for babies, but could also be used in coffee, cocoa, and various recipes. Canned milk offered real convenience to nineteenth-century America, where refrigeration was scarce. John Meyerberg, a Swiss immigrant, was the first to patent a process for condensing and canning milk without using sugar as a preservative. He named his company "Helvetia," the Latin word for Switzerland, and set up his first factory in Highland, Illinois, near St. Louis. Several other brands were produced by Helvetia, including one called "Our Pet," introduced in baby-sized cans in 1895. The brand was so popular the company was renamed the Pet Milk Company in 1923. Today, Pet, Inc., is a thriving and diversified company and Pet evaporated milk is still produced.

A baby's layette in the early 1900s might have included some of these brands of talcum powder. Manufacturers created special powders, and pictured babies on the packages to attract mothers' attention when shopping. Tiny-tot powder was produced by the United Drug Company, which later became the Rexall Company. The tin shown above is from the early 1920s. United Drug was founded in 1903 and, by 1907, had begun the nation's first chain of franchise drug stores. The Page Baby Talc tin was patented in 1914. Bonnie Babe talcum was offered by the Lane Bryant chain of retail stores. The company was started by Lena Himmelstein Bryant, a Lithuanian immigrant. She was a talented seamstress who had quite a following as she developed a line of maternity clothes, beginning in 1904. Maternity clothing was virtually nonexistent at that time, so women eagerly bought as many as she could make. The Lane Bryant name was actually a mistake—she accidentally established her first bank account with a misspelled deposit slip, but kept the name for her company. The firm later expanded into clothes for larger-sized women to meet her customers' requests. For a number of years, Lane Bryant offered layettes and, when twins or triplets arrived, gave additional layettes free to customers. The Lane Bryant name today appears on over 700 specialty stores for larger-sized women, but baby products are no longer carried.

The style of hat being worn by the baby on this pocket mirror helps date this advertising giveaway to the World War I era. The hat is a campaign-style four-dent crown, popular during that time period. Pocket mirrors were widely used in the first decade of this century to promote products and merchants. The mirrors were given to customers who undoubtedly used them often, seeing the advertisement again and again. The Harris-Polk Hat Company was organized in St. Louis, Missouri, in 1903 by Tyre C. Harris and William J. Polk. In 1939, the company merged with the eighty-year-old Langenberg Hat Company, also of St. Louis, to form the Harris-Langenberg Hat Company. Today, it is still possible to find hats carrying the Worth brand name made by the Langenberg Hat Company. The company is still located in St. Louis and makes a full range of men's and children's hats.

Products as varied as butter and chocolate candy give us the delightful images shown above. Fry's is credited with creating England's first chocolate candy bar. The company was started in 1728 by Walter Churchman, then Dr. Joseph Fry purchased the company in 1761. A series of sons and relatives entered the business and the company, then known as J. S. Fry & Sons, continued until 1952. Fry's became part of Cadbury, Ltd., in 1936, and Fry's chocolates are still sold in the United Kingdom. The ink blotter shown above is from about 1920. The Canadian butter pail for F. V. Vermette's Beurre Champlain is lithographed tin, and is typical of the way butter and peanut butter were packed in the early 1900s.

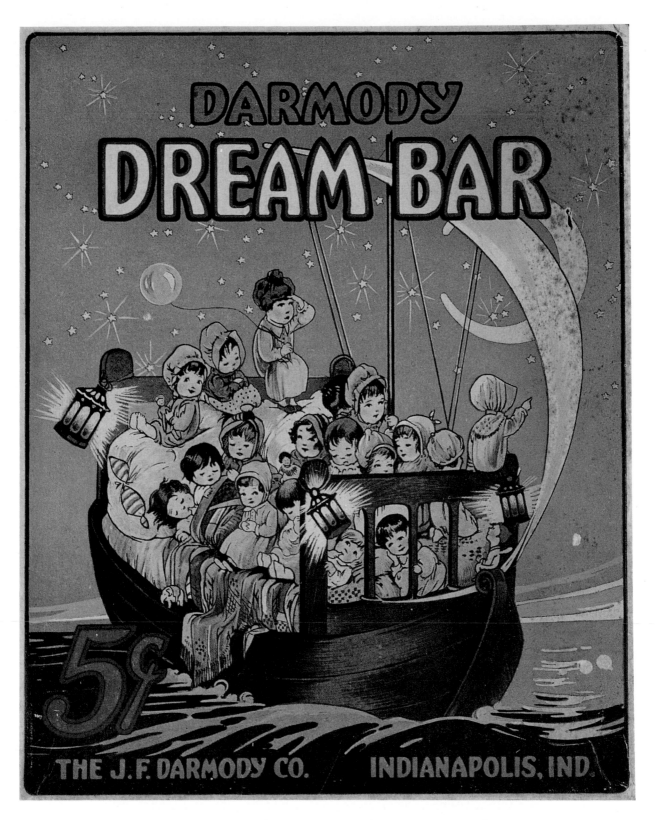

Store owners who received shipments of candy from the J. F. Darmody Company in the early years of this century must have admired this cute boatful of babies. The scene appeared on boxes that contained twenty-four Dream Bar candy bars. In addition to candy, the company sold extracts and bakers' supplies, as well as nuts, cigars, tobacco, and fancy groceries. This family-owned business began in 1895 and continued until 1941.

Appealing covers help sell magazines, and this cover illustration is especially attention-getting. Unfortunately, even when the public likes a magazine and circulation figures number into the hundreds of thousands, a magazine can disappear if competition is too great or advertising revenues are not large enough. *Today's Magazine* no longer exists. Popular illustrator Maud Tousey Fangel created the tender moment on this cover.

Parents are particular about babies' diets. The Ward Baking Company of Pittsburgh recognized this in portraying a charming baby with their bread on the 1921 advertising ink blotter shown at the right. Ward's slogan at the bottom, referring to health, also reinforced the connection between their product and well-being. The company was started in New York in 1849 by Hugh Ward, an Irish immigrant. A few years later he moved the company to Pittsburgh, Pennsylvania. The Ward Company had good reason for using a health theme in its advertising, because it is credited with building the nation's first modern sanitary bakery in Pittsburgh in 1903. Before that, most people baked their bread at home or carried their bread dough to public ovens. Ward pioneered baking and wrapping bread "untouched by human hands," as promoted in their advertising in the first decades of this century. And their "Clean Bread for New York" campaign in 1911 is said to have started a nationwide bakery cleanup effort. One of the company's most interesting campaigns occurred in 1914. Every month, a large, colorful billboard showing Ward's bread being made appeared in a number of major metropolitan areas. New York City celebrated its 300-year anniversary that year, and the Ward Company entered the tricentennial parade with a procession of sixty brand-new electric delivery trucks plus five floats, each carrying two of the marvelous outdoor posters used in their campaign. Ward's Bread was last made in 1980.

Union suits were the underwear of choice in the late 1800s and early 1900s. The Northwestern Knitting Company of Minneapolis chose these cute babies to model them for its Munsingwear brand. The Munsingwear trademark as shown here was used from about 1912 to 1920. George Munsing started the company in 1885, left it to pursue other interests in 1895, and returned to the firm in 1919, when the company name was officially changed to the Munsingwear Corporation. These die-cut cardboard signs were used in stores and display windows to promote the brand. Union suits declined in popularity and were discontinued in 1969. Today, Munsingwear, Inc., is a leading manufacturer of men's and women's undergarments, men's sportswear, and women's loungewear and sleepwear.

Compliments of

G. F. FROST,
LEXINGTON STREET,
Cor. Mass. Cen. R. R.   Moody St., Cor. F. R. R.

Coal, Wood, Hay, Lime,
CEMENT, BRICK,
Drain Pipe, Sand, Plaster, Hair, &c.

2007

WALTHAM, MASS.

This beautiful Victorian-era die-cut was given away by G. F. Frost, the proprietor of a wholesale/retail coal and construction supply house in Waltham, Massachusetts. The company was started in 1855 and Frost acquired it in 1882. He was able to ship materials easily to other parts of the state as his property bordered the tracks of both the Fitchburg Railroad and the Massachusetts Central Railroad. The business prospered and, by 1893, Frost had a total of nineteen employees to handle the large number of orders he received. Frost's company continued until 1909.

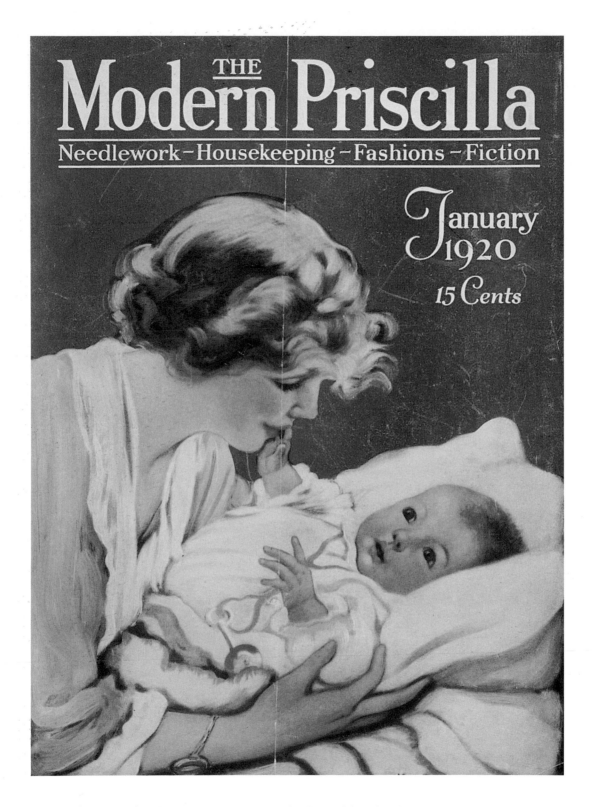

Katharine Richardson Wireman painted this beautiful and realistic nursery scene. Her illustrations were popular during the early 1900s, and could often be seen on the covers of magazines such as *Scribner's*, *The Ladies' Home Journal*, *Collier's*, and *The Saturday Evening Post*. She also created magazine ads for the Cream of Wheat Company. Wireman was born in 1878 and always signed her work with initials rather than her first name. *The Modern Priscilla* magazine was one of a number of women's publications that deemphasized fashion around the turn of the century and emphasized activities, fiction, and home arts. Originally published in 1887 in Lynn, Massachusetts, it was moved to Boston in 1894 and achieved a healthy circulation before its demise in 1930.

THE PEOPLE'S HOME JOURNAL

JANUARY, 1918   TEN CENTS

The Wooing o' Jean

Mary Imlay Taylor's Great Romantic Novel

"Weighing the Baby"   J. F. KERNAN

F. M. LUPTON, *Publisher*, NEW YORK

"We all drink cocoa!" is the translation of the wording printed around this beautifully lithographed German cocoa tin. The container is unusual because the knobbed lid fits tightly, creating a reusable canister. The product that came packed inside the tin was made by the Von Jordan & Timmeaus company, most probably in the heyday of lithographed tin advertising—around the turn of the century.

Proud parents who keep track of their baby's vital statistics may be able to imagine themselves in this illustration titled "Weighing the Baby." During the early 1900s, general stores had scales, such as the one depicted here, that were used for weighing produce and other items. A baby probably was weighed in, as well, every now and then. *The People's Home Journal* was a magazine for women that published articles about homemaking as well as fiction stories from 1886 to 1929.

The makers of Murray & Lanman's Florida Water surrounded their product's bottle with fantasy cherubs on this 1894 advertising card. Florida Water became a generic name for a type of cologne around the turn of the century. The New York firm of Lanman and Kemp defended their Florida Water as "the original and genuine article" and urged consumers not to be deceived by "worthless or inferior articles generally sold as Florida Water." The formula for Florida Water contained the oils of lavender, orange, and cloves, as well as musk and alcohol. The product was advertised both as a scented toilet water and as a medical product for reviving a patient in case of "fever, nausea, lassitude, and faintness." Murray & Lanman's Florida Water is no longer made.

American women were enthusiastic users of sewing machines during the late 1880s. Even today, many people can still recall childhood memories of watching Mother sew. This illustration is from a Singer Manufacturing Co. booklet that was given away at the Pan-American Exposition in Buffalo, New York, in 1901. That was almost fifty years after Isaac Merritt Singer sold his first sewing machine. Singer did not invent the sewing machine, but his improvements to the types of machines already in existence finally made them practical for home use. Singer advertised that the only difference between the least expensive Singer machine and the most expensive one was the cabinetwork and ornamentation. All machines were equally reliable and capable of producing the finest work. Today, millions of people continue to use Singer machines.

The "fadeaway" style of illustration shown above was developed by Coles Phillips, a popular American artist in the first few decades of this century. His earlier work was mainly of stylized, beautiful young women—"fantasy women" as they were called at the time. In this advertisement, the mother and baby show Phillips's later style, mirroring reality. Phillips illustrated advertisements for products as diverse as silver plate, paint, and pharmaceuticals. His work was most often seen, though, on the covers of popular magazines of his time, including *The Saturday Evening Post*, *Good Housekeeping*, and *Life*. Luxite Textiles, Inc., went out of business in 1926, but the company's beautiful advertisements featuring "Phillips Girls" are prized by collectors today.

These babies are the picture of health, perfect symbols of the benefits of eating the brands of food products they promoted. Hecker's Buckwheat Baby is a die-cut advertising card from the late 1800s, given away by the Hecker-Jones-Jewell Milling Company of New York. Although the baby is a bit young to eat such a hefty breakfast, the beautiful artwork of baby wielding a knife and fork is certainly attention-getting. The Hecker's brand dates back to the 1840s.

The baby below grins out from a label made for the end of a wooden fruit crate around 1920. At that time, fruit was shipped from growers to distributors in wooden boxes, and every brand had a colorful label for identification. The Andrews Brothers company was started around 1900 and continues in business today. The Buddy brand, used for oranges as well as apples, is no longer produced.

56

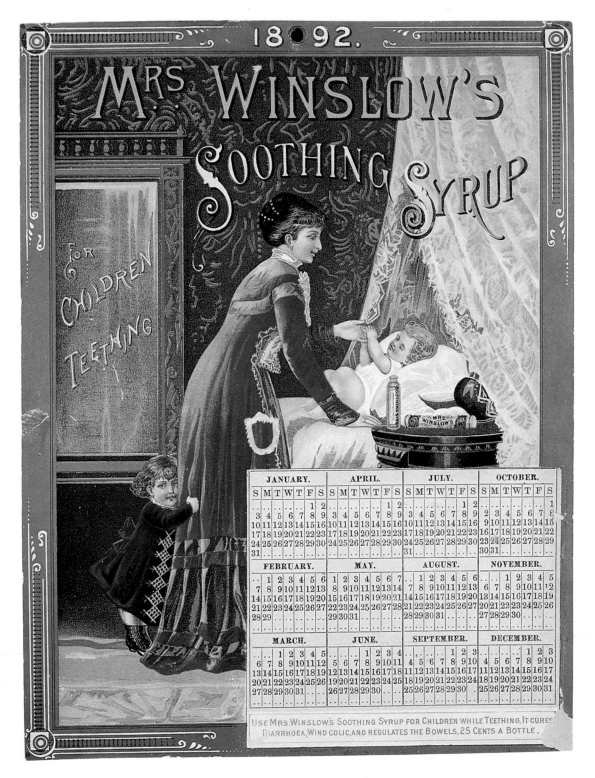

Advertising for Mrs. Winslow's Soothing Syrup, such as this beautiful calendar, was directed toward mothers who wanted to ease discomfort felt by their teething children. The product was advertised just after the turn of the century as a tried-and-true remedy for over sixty years. It was supposed to "soothe the child, soften the gums, allay all pain, cure wind colic, and remedy diarrhea." Many such over-the-counter patent medicines were sold by druggists as modern medications in the late 1800s, before the Food and Drug Act passed in 1906. According to pharmacy records of the time, Mrs. Winslow's Soothing Syrup contained spirit of fennel, water, sugar, syrup, sodium carbonate, and morphine sulphate! It was offered by the Winslow Chemical Company of New York, and later by the Anglo-American Chemical Company (without the morphine).

Kewpies captured the hearts of Americans beginning in 1909, when the first Kewpie illustration appeared in *The Ladies' Home Journal*. Their creator, Rose O'Neill, said her baby brother was the inspiration for these fantasy creatures, named Kewpies because that was a diminutive term for Cupid. Kewpie-illustrated pages became a regular feature in the *Woman's Home Companion* in September 1910, with Kewpies entertaining Dotty Darling, the youngest child in a make-believe family who had no playmates. Kewpies were so popular that soon there were Kewpie toys, dolls, writing paper, greeting cards (such as the one shown above, top left), and even Kewpie wallpaper.

Kewpies endorsed a number of products in advertising. Kewpie Corn (*opposite page, top*) was a product of the Mammoth Spring Canning Company of Sussex, Wisconsin. The company was started in 1920 by John "J. P." Kraemer and a group of local businessmen. The company mainly produced vegetables for private-label brands, but the main proprietary brand was Kewpie. The label on the can shown is one of the last designs produced, dating the can between 1950 and 1965. The company was sold in 1966 and this brand is no longer produced.

The beautiful booklet at the left was offered by the Genessee Pure Food Company of LeRoy, New York, to promote Jell-O. Kewpies are seen frolicking throughout its pages as well as helping the little "Jell-O girl" on the front cover. Peter Cooper received a patent for a gelatin dessert as early as 1845, but no one marketed the product until cough syrup manufacturer Pearl B. Wait adapted Cooper's recipe in 1897. His wife came up with the catchy name of Jell-O. In 1899, O. F. Woodward bought the rights to Jell-O for just $450. Today, JELL-O is a product of Kraft General Foods, Inc., and a dessert enjoyed by millions of people.

The unusual store display shown below was eye-catching and appealing to shoppers in the heyday of Kewpie popularity. It measures approximately 12″ square and the Kewpie on top adds another 9½″ in height. Arthur Frankenstein & Co. of New York advertised Kewpie Garters extensively in women's magazines of the time. Kewpie Garters are no longer made.

Advertising cards like the one above were given out to customers of general stores in the 1880s and 1890s. This one must have brought a smile to farmers who were beginning to enjoy the labor-saving benefits of farm machinery made possible by companies like William Deering & Company of Chicago. Deering was a New England merchant who, in the 1870s, invested in a struggling farm-equipment business that made harvesters—new machines that challenged the famous reaper invented by Cyrus McCormick. After years of rivalry, the Deering and McCormick companies combined on July 28, 1902, to become the International Harvester Company. Today, the company is Navistar International Corporation.

This baby was so charming that the Nabisco company used the image over and over again in advertising during a thirty-year period. All that changed was the box design. The scene was originally painted in 1916 by Pearl Hill, a staff artist for the National Biscuit Company. The company featured the baby in print advertising, store display cards, and even a carton insert. As the package design changed, the company simply adapted the artwork to include the revised box. The version shown here is from the late 1940s. Graham Crackers bear the name of the man who invented them in 1829—Sylvester Graham. Near the turn of the century, the National Biscuit Company improved the manufacturing process, leading to the mass production of Graham Crackers and to their widespread popularity. The modern company, Nabisco Brands, Inc., dates back to 1792, when the Pearson & Sons bakery was established in Newburyport, Massachusetts. Today, millions of boxes of Nabisco Graham Crackers are sold every year.

VIVAUDOU'S

MAVIS

TALC

for the family—
Even baby knows
how good it is

Paris VIVAUDOU New York

62

This memorable advertisement helped Pears' Soap become one of England's most prominent brands. It was used in both British and American magazines in the early years of this century. The Pears company dates back to 1789, when Andrew Pears, a hairdresser, moved from Cornwall to London. He became popular with wealthy Londoners and soon began to experiment with making soap that would be gentle to the skin. From the beginning, he advertised extensively, and the soap was a tremendous success. But it wasn't until nearly one hundred years later, when Thomas Barratt joined the company, that Pears began a promotional campaign that was unequaled in British history. His creativity is seen in the ad above, and there were many, many more ads, advertising cards, promotional giveaways, and even endorsements by celebrities and royalty to bring awareness of the Pears' name. Pears' Soap is still one of the leading brands in England. Since 1958, A & F Pears Limited has sponsored the "Miss Pears" contest for girls between the ages of three and nine, and crowns a new winner each year selected from thousands of photographs entered by proud parents.

Babies and small children can be extremely creative when left alone for just a moment! This mischievous little tyke appeared in a 1923 magazine advertisement for Mavis Talc. The Vivadou company produced a series of ads by popular illustrators during the 1920s. Mavis Talc was first introduced in 1915 and is still produced today by American-International Industries.

What are these Babies after?

LACTATED FOOD.

IT MAKES THEM HEALTHY, HAPPY, HEARTY!
THAT'S WHY THEY LOVE IT.
PAMPHLET FREE. WELLS, RICHARDSON & CO., BURLINGTON, VT.

150 MEALS FOR $1.00

At the turn of the century, Wells, Richardson & Co. spent over $500,000 a year to promote its products—a phenomenal budget at the time and not a small amount even by today's standards. These advertising cards are examples of the beautiful color lithography the company used to show babies made healthy by drinking their Lactated Food product. It was a milk substitute, said to be more easily digested and more nourishing than milk alone. At the height of its success, the company received nearly two thousand letters per day from satisfied customers, including parents and doctors endorsing Lactated Food. The company's business declined when the Food and Drug Act of 1906 began requiring companies to disclose the presence of narcotics in their products. Unfortunately, Wells, Richardson & Co.'s best seller—Paine's Celery Compound—contained cocaine. The company finally went out of business in 1943, but Lactated Food brand was sold to Sterling Drug, Inc., in 1922. Lactated Food is no longer made.

THESE AND THOUSANDS OF OTHER BABIES
HAVE BEEN NOURISHED AND HAVE GROWN STRONG ON
ESKAY'S FOOD

The infant-formula market was quite competitive in the last years of the nineteenth century. Two other prominent products were Eskay's Food and Mellin's Food. Eskay's was manufactured by Smith, Kline & French. The company bought the rights to make the product in 1896 from Frank Baum, a Philadelphia druggist who had created what he called "Albumenized Food." The Eskay's product was described on each bottle as "a mixture of milk, sugar, scientifically prepared cereals, egg, and inorganic salts for modifying cow's milk, making a most palatable, digestible and nutritious food for infants." Eskay's was the brand name used for various Smith, Kline & French specialty products. The advertising postcard above is from the early 1900s.

Mellin's Food was the leading British brand at the turn of the century, so it is not surprising that American businessmen would find a way to bring distribution of it to the United States. Like Eskay's Food, Mellin's was also added to fresh milk to create a ready-to-use formula. The magazine ad at the left appeared on the back cover of *The Youth's Companion* in October 1899. The colorful die-cut advertising giveaway is from the same era. The ad and die-cut were from The Mellin Food Company of Boston, but at the time of the World's Columbian Exposition in Chicago in 1893, the Doliber-Goodale Co. of Boston was marketing the product. In fact, Mellin's was used to feed infants being cared for at the fair's children's building. Neither Eskay's nor Mellin's is available today in the United States.

These babies' expressions are as cute today as they were in the 1950s, when the babies posed for the photographer's camera. Cry Baby and Miss Seedless Grapes were sold by the Anthony Guerriero fruit company of Fresno, California. The owner's son, Joe, is featured on the Cry Baby label, and their daughter, Ginger, smiles from the Miss Seedless one. The Cry Baby brand was introduced in 1953; the Miss Seedless brand was first sold in 1955. Both brands are Thompson Seedless table grapes, but the Miss Seedless variety was also used to make juice. Both brands are still available. Grapes were among the first kinds of fruit shipped east from California in the 1880s. Fruit was shipped in wooden boxes to protect it from being crushed, and colorful labels were affixed to the ends of the crates to identify each grower's brand. Grape crates were flatter than other fruit crates, so their labels were typically about 4″ high × 13″ wide instead of the square shape used for other fruits.

This magazine ad from the 1930s appeared over sixty years after Dr. Israel W. Lyon began developing his line of oral hygiene products. He had studied in New York and then practiced dentistry in California during the Gold Rush of the 1850s. By 1866, he returned east and introduced tooth tablets, a tooth cleanser in solid cake form, packaged in a small metal box. The tablets were made of chalk, orris root, and castile soap, and came with a small tool for cutting individual "tablets" to apply to a wet toothbrush. In 1874, tooth powder was introduced. His dental cream was available as early as 1879 and sold until the 1950s. Dr. Lyon's dental products contained no alcohol, and his advertising never made false claims. A drawing of Dr. Lyon's wife, Pamela, appeared on the packaging in 1866 and continued as a trademark until the last of the Dr. Lyon products—tooth powder—was discontinued in the 1960s. The business was acquired by Sterling Drug Inc. in 1934.

"I insist upon a *pure dentifrice* for my child just as much as *pure milk*. I want his teeth white and clean and I don't take any chances with them."

Dr. Lyon's
DENTAL CREAM

"BRIGHT EYES"

1923	JANUARY	1923

Calendars are tried-and-true sales promotion items, and the illustration is often the key to its success. So, if people like the illustration—such as this darling baby—they are likely to use the calendar throughout the year. The sales message, then, is seen many times. Cascara Bromide Quinine was a popular medicine for cold symptoms and was sold by the W. H. Hill Company during the late 1800s and early 1900s. William H. Hill started the company in 1885 when he moved to Detroit. He was a doctor's son who had been a traveling pharmaceuticals salesman. He studied at night to learn pharmacy and chemistry, and the medications he developed were sold all over the United States as well as in Canada and Europe. This calendar was produced the year before Hill retired and sold the company. CBQ tablets are no longer made.

Another kind of calendar was made by E. W. Hoyt & Co. of Lowell, Massachusetts. To promote their German Cologne, the company liberally applied it to advertising cards like the one at the right. A full-year calendar was printed on the back. Every time the calendar was used, the fragrance of the cologne served as a product reminder. Hoyt's made these early "pocket" calendars in a variety of designs, including many lovely images of babies and small children. This one was from 1896. Because large numbers of German immigrants were living in America at the time, the German Cologne was quite popular; in fact, it was considered good luck to wear it. Rubifoam was Hoyt's dental cleanser. It was usually advertised along with the cologne during this era, but it is no longer made. Hoyt's Cologne, however, is still produced by J. Strickland & Company. It is sold all over the United States and in fourteen other countries.

This beautifully illustrated tin serving tray is an unusually artistic example of early twentieth-century patent medicine advertising. It was made for the Capudine Chemical Company by the H. D. Beach Company of Coshocton, Ohio, an early printing concern known for producing outstanding colorful tin advertising items such as lithographed signs and trays. The tray may have been used for serving or hung on a wall as an advertisement in either a general store or a pharmacy. The wording on the top of the box indicates that Capudine did not contain narcotics such as opium, cocaine, heroin, or morphine. This helps date the tray to after 1906, when the federal Food and Drug Act required that such ingredients be disclosed on the product package. In 1899, Henry T. Hicks established his first business in Raleigh, North Carolina, to sell pharmaceuticals, toilet articles, and garden seed. The Capudine Chemical Company was formed in 1904 and continued until its dissolution in 1961. Hicks was also associated with several pharmacies in Raleigh through the 1920s.

AFTER
THE BATH.

Dainty clothes and tender skin
Need pure soap to wash them in.
Nurse and mother must be sure
Baby's bath is sweet and pure.

A child fresh from its bath in clean dainty clothes
is a suggestion of Ivory Soap. All dainty wash-
able things may be restored to their original
freshness without injury, by use of Ivory Soap.

The ornate talcum powder tin at right was reproduced by A. A. Vantine & Company of New York. In the early years of this century, women who purchased this brand may have been attracted to the beauty of the packaging. But there were many talcum powders being marketed in beautiful tins and it's more likely that a mother would be influenced by the idea of providing her baby with a sanitary powder for its sensitive skin. A. A. Vantine & Company went out of business in 1942.

The Procter & Gamble Company produced the lovely magazine insert at the left in 1899. At that time, most magazines were printed only in black and white, but separately printed colorful advertising inserts could be bound into them. Procter & Gamble promoted sales of their Ivory brand of soap by offering a reproduction of the illustration, without the wording, as a print suitable for framing. All the customer needed to do was send in ten soap wrappers. This insert was one of a series of Ivory Soap ads that offered framable prints as premiums. The artist who created the original "After the Bath" painting was Irving Ramsey Wiles. He was a celebrated illustrator whose portraiture, usually done in transparent watercolors, reproduced beautifully in magazines. Procter & Gamble was founded in Cincinnati in 1837 and Ivory Soap was introduced in 1879.

Paper dolls have amused children for many years, and some of the cutest of these have been paper dolls of babies. Perhaps the most famous series was Dolly Dingle, drawn by Grace G. Drayton, which appeared in *Pictorial Review* between 1916 and 1933. Dolly Dingle's Baby Brother was introduced in June 1916. Grace Drayton is best known for her chubby children, the Campbell Kids, who appeared in Campbell's Soup advertising for many decades.

Paper doll "families" that appeared in women's magazines stayed interesting month after month because the artist introduced new characters and situations. The Twins by Frances Tipton Hunter were paper dolls that grew older as the series progressed, allowing not only new clothes but also several different dolls as they "grew up." The page shown appeared in 1923 in *Woman's Home Companion*.

Betty Bonnet's Sister's Baby
By Sheila Young

NOTE—If the whole page is mounted on muslin or linen before the figures are cut out the different parts will last longer and the tabs will not tear so easily. Cut along the dotted lines, and slip the doll's head into the slits thus made. By pasting an inch-wide strip of cardboard at the waistline, slightly bent to form an easel, the doll can be made to stand.

Sheila Young created the Betty Bonnet series of paper dolls in 1915. Betty Bonnet's Sister's Baby appeared in the October 1916 issue of *The Ladies' Home Journal*. These monthly doll pages, which continued until 1918, had an amazing amount of detail and included many interesting accessories, giving insight into the lifestyles of the time. The Betty Bonnet series showed an affluent family, as evidenced here by the elaborate layette and child's pony cart. Betty Bonnet was the second of Young's paper doll characters. The Lettie Lane series began in 1908 and continued until 1915, when Lettie introduced Betty to all her friends in the magazine's audience.

Pianos were important sources of entertainment in the days before radio and television. Of course, not everyone could play the piano or read sheet music, so player pianos could be found in many households. The die-cut baby at left from 1917 was the company symbol for the Gulbransen-Dickinson Co. of Chicago. This baby was usually shown pushing on the pedals to demonstrate the ease of playing the Gulbransen brand of piano. The company began producing player pianos in 1907 and continued until 1932. Regular piano operations were discontinued in 1971. Today, Gulbransen is a world-renowned manufacturer of digital musical instrument products, including digital home organs and acoustic pianos.

Talented composers have written so many songs about babies that it is hard to select just a few to single out for mention. The mid-nineteenth-century song sheets at the left were found in bound volumes of sheet music from that era. "Slumber on Baby dear" was published in 1863 and "Baby Mine" in 1875. The composer of "Slumber on Baby dear," L. M. Gottschalk, was one of the most celebrated composer/piano musicians in America from the mid-1840s until the 1860s. He received much acclaim in Europe as well, and was so popular women were said to actually swoon at his concerts.

This fruit crate label, first used in 1918, gets an A in design because it is so attractive and attention-getting. Such beautiful labels were first used in the late 1800s, and continued into the 1940s and 1950s to identify brands of fruit from particular growers and growers' associations. The labels were glued to the ends of wooden boxes in which fruit was packed for shipment from the West to customers in the East. The Villa Park Orchards Association belonged to the California Fruit Growers Exchange, which first used the Sunkist trademark in advertising and packaging in 1908. Labels first featured the tissue-wrapped Sunkist orange in 1917. In addition to oranges, Villa Park Orchards Association also packs grapefruit and tangerines. The Sunkist brand appears only on premium-quality fruit.

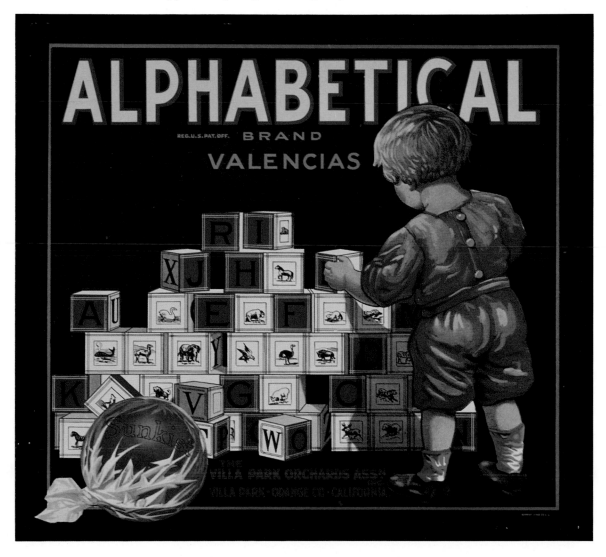

Undoubtedly, the scenes shown on this cardboard
advertising sign from the late 1800s were intended to make
men do a double-take—or a triple-take! Tobacco
companies used all sorts of advertising during that era to
get men's attention, and there were hundreds of competing
brands. The Marburg Brothers Tobacco Company of
Baltimore, Maryland, manufactured smoking tobacco during
and after the Civil War, and into the 1930s. North Carolina
was one of the leading tobacco-growing areas in the United
States, and that may have inspired early marketers at
Marburg Brothers to feature North Carolina prominently on
the company's tobacco packages.

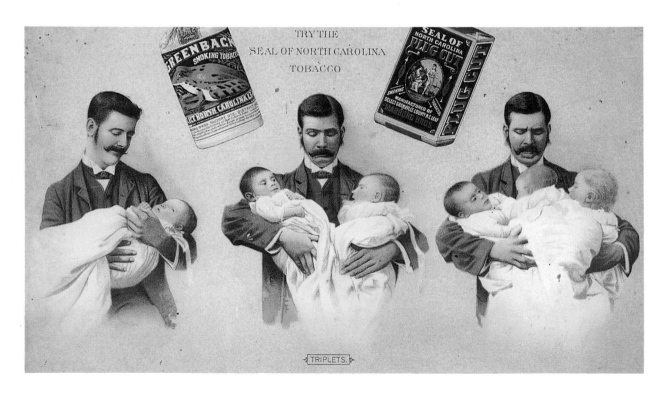

The "Fairy Tree" is really a charming British biscuit container made in 1935. William Crawford & Sons, Ltd., biscuit manufacturers, commissioned popular artists of the time to design a special series of decorative tins. The unusual Fairy Tree was created by Mabel Lucie Attwell, a prominent artist whose illustrations of highly stylized children were eagerly sought by the public. Attwell's daughter, Peggy, was the inspiration for many of her toddler characters, pictured on postcards, on chinaware, and in children's books. The Fairy Tree tin also functioned as a savings bank for children. There is a money slot at the back, and the cone-shaped top can be removed. Crawford's biscuits are still produced in England by United Biscuits (UK) Limited.

The Cream of Wheat Company commissioned some of the most renowned artists of the day to illustrate its advertising in the early years of this century. Edward V. Brewer (1883–1971) created approximately 102 paintings for Cream of Wheat ads between 1911 and 1926. Cream of Wheat was first produced in the 1890s as a "breakfast porridge" experiment by a group of men who owned a flour mill in Grand Fork, North Dakota. Since this product was made from a part of the wheat considered to be the best quality, it was named Cream of Wheat. Its immediate sales success caused the company to seek larger quarters in 1897, and it was moved to Minneapolis—a more central location for shipping. A black chef has been the company's trademark since the first packages were shipped. The chef, as shown in these examples, was dubbed "Rastus" and appeared throughout the years after being introduced in the early 1900s. The Cream of Wheat Company became part of the National Biscuit Company in 1961, which today is Nabisco Brands, Inc.

Painted by Edw. V. Brewer for Cream of Wheat Co.   Copyright 1922 by Cream of Wheat Co.
"WHERE HEALTHY BABIES COME FROM"

"HERE YOU ARE."

Painted by Edward V. Brewer for Cream of Wheat Co.   Copyright 1917 by Cream of Wheat Co.

1 · 9 · 2 · 3

"STARTING THE NEW YEAR RIGHT"

Painted by Edw. V. Brewer for Cream of Wheat Company   *Copyright 1922 by Cream of Wheat Company*

THE A B C CLASS.

Beautiful babies and very young children were often found on patent medicine advertising. Manufacturers hoped people would associate the youthful charm and healthy appearance of children with the use of their product. Hood's remedies, produced by the C. I. Hood Company, included Sarsaparilla and Vegetable Pills, which were promoted by the two advertising cards shown above. Sarsaparilla claimed to purify the blood—a popular medical theory during the late 1800s. The product supposedly cured everything from indigestion to malaria. Hood's Vegetable Pills was a laxative, promoted as "after-dinner pills" that removed bowel obstructions! Charles Ira Hood developed the Sarsaparilla product while a pharmacist in Lowell, Massachusetts. He went on to open a drug factory there in 1882. Within a decade, he was producing 25 million pieces of advertising each year, including colorful advertising cards and other customer premiums the whole family could enjoy. These included game and coloring books, puzzles, paper dolls, calendars, and cookbooks—liberally sprinkled with advertising messages. The Warner-Lambert Company acquired the rights to the Hood's name in the twentieth century, but the products have not been made for many years.

Jujube candies can be found in various shapes, but Jujube Dolls were offered exclusively by the Henry Heide candy company in the early 1900s. Assorted fruit flavors of that popular gelatinlike candy were packed in this delightful five-pound box for shipment to retail stores. There were 205 Jujube Dolls per pound. The company also made pink and white Marshmallow Dolls during this same time period. Henry Heide came to America from Germany in 1866 and began to manufacture candies in New York City in 1869. His high-quality candies were an immediate success. By the time his Jujube Dolls were being produced, the company employed almost nine hundred people in four huge buildings and the candy was being sold around the world. Heide's moved to new manufacturing facilities in New Jersey in 1962 and today produces a number of popular sweets, including Licorice Drops, Jelly Beans, Candy Corn, Cinnamon Bears, Jujyfruits, and Jujubes. The company claims to be the first to offer Jujube candies. Jujube Dolls, however, are no longer made.

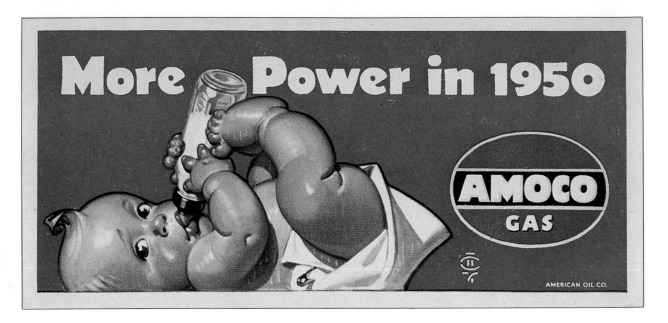

After World War II, manufacturers resumed automobile production, which had been suspended so tanks and other military goods could be made. As soldiers returned home to a normal way of life, families were started and cars became necessities. Gasoline companies stepped up advertising, competing for consumer attention with new slogans and the offering of premiums. This ink blotter from the American Oil Company featured an illustration by J. C. Leyendecker, one of America's most popular illustrators in the first few decades of this century. His art was seen on magazine covers and in advertisements for Arrow shirts, Kellogg's cereals, and Kuppenheimer clothing, to name a few. The American Oil Company merged with Indiana Standard Oil Company in 1925. Today, the company is part of a diversified corporation known by the name of the brand advertised on this ink blotter—Amoco. The Amoco Corporation is one of the world's leading producers of petroleum and chemical products.

When much of America was engaged in the business of farming, publications like *Capper's Farmer* were important periodicals with large circulations. The whimsical drawing on the cover of this March 1933 issue was created by Charles Twelvetrees, a popular artist of the time. Not much is known about Twelvetrees, as he led a rather reclusive life, but his illustrations charmed millions of people who purchased them on postcards, magazine covers, and greeting cards. *Capper's Farmer* began in 1893 as the *Missouri Valley Farmer* in Atchison, Kansas. Arthur Capper published a number of other agricultural publications, including *Kansas Farmer*, similar magazines in Ohio, Pennsylvania, and Michigan, and *Capper's Weekly*, a rural opinion and news journal. Capper was later a U.S. senator from Kansas.

Capper's Farmer

Vol. 44—No. 3   5 Cents a Copy   March, 1933

This Order is Good for One Bar of BIG MASTER SOAP. (See other side.)

Babies played a large role in promoting soaps made by Lautz Bros. & Co. of New York in the late 1800s. The image at the left was used extensively on advertising cards. The baby above also appeared on wrappers of Big Master Soap bars. The Lautz brothers—J. Adam, Charles, and Frederick—were German immigrants who took over and expanded a soap-making business started by their father, William, in 1853. The company became Lautz Bros. & Co. in 1866 when William Lautz died. The brothers also had interests in a number of other Buffalo, New York, businesses, including the Niagara Marble Works and the Niagara Starch Works. The Lautz families continued the business into the 1920s. The coupon above is from 1899 and has a two-for-one offer on the back. A bar of Big Master Soap was given free with the purchase of another bar of any brand of Lautz Bros. soap or Snow Boy washing powder.

Dutch designer and illustrator Henriette Willebeck LeMair (1889–1966) created the charming family scene at right for Colgate & Co.'s FAB Soap Flakes magazine advertising in 1923. The artist, whose style was influenced by a trip to the Middle East when she was young, signed her works "Saida." She is best known for her illustrations in children's books and her work can be seen in the children's chapel of one of Holland's beautiful cathedrals. Colgate's FAB Soap Flakes was popular for washing delicate items (including babies!). The FAB brand name is still in use today, on a detergent that was introduced in 1947 by the Colgate-Palmolive Company.

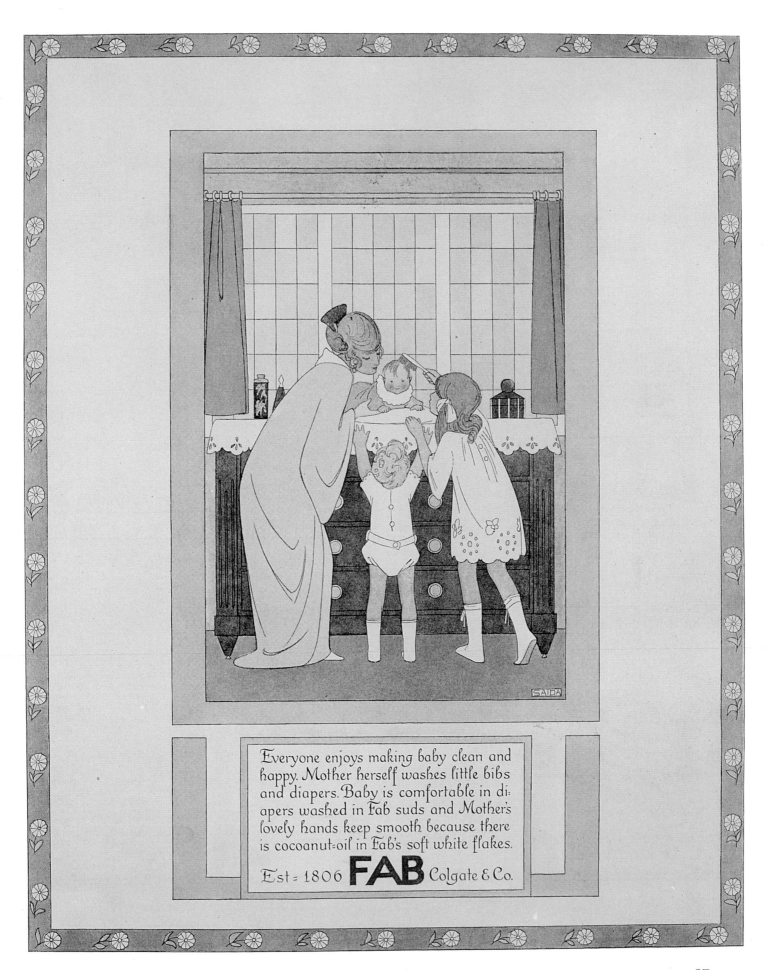

Tobacco companies and cigar manufacturers of the late 1800s and early 1900s counted on beautiful imagery—rather than substantive claims— to promote their brands. The Young Fritz Cigar sign is die-cut cardboard and a good example of how colorful, realistic art can capture consumer attention. The lithography is so beautiful, it's hard to believe it is approximately a century old! There were literally thousands of brands of cigars made during this time period, so differentiating a brand was of the utmost importance in building a following. Although no information was found about the company that produced the Young Fritz brand, it's likely the name and image were intended to honor someone in particular, such as a child, relative, or friend of the company's owner.

The Johnson & Johnson company had already made a name for itself as an innovator in medicinal products when it introduced Johnson's baby powder in 1893. So, undoubtedly, the baby powder was well received by physicians and mothers alike. In 1886, the Johnson brothers—Robert W., James W., and Edward M.—went into business to manufacture medicinal plasters. At the time, hospital operating rooms were usually unsanitary, with doctors operating ungloved and wearing smocks over street clothes. The Johnsons developed antiseptic surgical dressings and even a surgical procedures handbook in 1888 that became a standard for antiseptic practices. By 1892, they had developed sterile manufacturing procedures. The company's scientific director was Fred B. Kilmer, whose son was the famous poet Joyce Kilmer. "The Jury of Babies" ink blotter and the paper die-cut in-store display piece shown at the right date to the 1920-to-mid-1930s period. Today, Johnson & Johnson is an international family of over 170 companies marketing health-care products in over 150 countries.

PICTORIAL REVIEW

Spring
Fashion
Number

Beginning a New Serial
"The Prairie Mother"
By
ARTHUR STRINGER

APRIL 1920   TWENTY-FIVE CENTS

Among the many baby powders mothers could buy in the 1920s and '30s were the Baby and Baby Mine brands shown above. Lander Perfumers began in 1920 in Binghamton, New York. Charles Ostreich and his employer, Elliott Carter, a New York manufacturer, invested in a cosmetic business belonging to Carter's cousin—a Mr. Loveland. A second company was formed, which they named by combining the last syllables of the cousins' names. Ostreich ran the business, eventually bought out his partners, and developed the company into a multimillion-dollar low-priced cosmetics and toiletries business. Today, the Lander Company, Inc., sells a wide variety of personal-care products. Baby Mine powder was sold under the Zanol name, made by the American Products Company of Cincinnati, Ohio. There were six Zanol talcum powders produced, but only Baby Mine was marketed directly to mothers of infants. In addition to toiletries, the company produced a line of flavor extracts, soft drink extracts, and soaps. The American Products Company was founded in 1907 and continued into the late 1940s.

A heartwarming illustration by artist Torre Bevans greeted subscribers to *Pictorial Review* magazine in April 1920 (*left*). It is the dream-come-true concept of a child finding the Easter Bunny that makes this artwork as timely today as it was then. *Pictorial Review* was one of America's most popular magazines in the 1920s and 1930s. It was well-known for publishing short stories by popular writers and for pioneering informative columns about medical issues. William Randolph Hearst bought the magazine in 1934 and combined it with another large-circulating women's magazine, *The Delineator*, in 1937. Due to declining advertising revenues, however, it ceased publication in 1939.

America's Sleepheart

Sleep like a Kitten   *arrive Fresh as a Daisy*

1937		JANUARY				1937
SUN	MON	TUE	WED	THU	FRI	SAT
					1	2
3	4	5	6	7	8	9
10	11	12	13	14	15	16
17	18	19	20	21	22	23
24 31	25	26	27	28	29	30

1937		FEBRUARY			1937	
SUN	MON	TUE	WED	THU	FRI	SAT
	1	2	3	4	5	6
7	8	9	10	11	12	13
14	15	16	17	18	19	20
21	22	23	24	25	26	27
28						

1937		MARCH				1937
SUN	MON	TUE	WED	THU	FRI	SAT
	1	2	3	4	5	6
7	8	9	10	11	12	13
14	15	16	17	18	19	20
21	22	23	24	25	26	27
28	29	30	31			

THE GEORGE WASHINGTON

CHESAPEAKE and OHIO *Lines*

Original Predecessor Company Founded by George Washington in 1785.

THE SPORTSMAN · THE F.F.V.

THE FINEST FLEET OF GENUINELY AIR-CONDITIONED TRAINS IN THE WORLD

The Chesapeake and Ohio railroad combined two sure winners in an effort to attract attention with this 1937 calendar. The railroad introduced "Chessie" the cat in 1933 in a campaign to promote overnight travel via air-conditioned sleeper cars. The slogan the snoozing Chessie personified was "Sleep like a Kitten, arrive Fresh as a Daisy." Chessie was so popular that a series of calendars was introduced in 1934, and this 1937 calendar added a baby for extra attention-getting power. Chesapeake and Ohio became the CSX Corporation.

The artist who created the magazine cover at the right, Maud Tousey Fangel, insisted on drawing babies from live models, but unfortunately no record could be found to identify this baby or mother. This early style of her art from 1913 is more realistic than the later pastels which are more recognizable as her work (some examples are on pages 13 and 37). *The Ladies' Home Journal* began when Cyrus Curtis published a women's section in his *Tribune and Farmer* publication in 1879. Supposedly, his wife laughed at his efforts to target a female audience and he challenged her to try editing the section herself. She did, and was so successful that the whole publication prospered—allowing the Curtises to buy out a partner and form the Curtis Publishing Company in 1884. The magazine catered to women's changing interests over the years, including in its many departments everything from popular fiction to home-building plans and health advice. Of course, women's fashions, beauty tips, and home decorating ideas were always included as well. Today, *Ladies' Home Journal* continues as one of the most widely read magazines in America.

THE
LADIES' HOME
JOURNAL
CHRISTMAS
1913

PAINTED BY MAUD TOUSEY FANGEL

FIFTEEN CENTS · THE CURTIS PUBLISHING COMPANY PHILADELPHIA

This valentine shows the surprising realism and beauty that characterized items produced by Rafael Tuck & Sons, Ltd. Tuck printed some of the most beautiful postcards, greeting cards, paper dolls, and bookplates of the late 1800s and early 1900s. Born in Germany, Tuck set up a print shop in London in 1866. The company expanded rapidly as the public's demand for the brilliantly colored lithography extended into other countries, including the United States. "Love's Message" was designed at the firm's New York studios, then printed at the Fine Art Works in Saxony. The Tuck company is still in existence but its early printing plates were destroyed in 1940 during a German bombing raid.

A bundle of joy for the New Year was an appropriate subject for the cover of this 1911 magazine. It was painted by Clara M. Burd, who had a talent for drawing babies as well as beautiful decorative borders (some can be seen on several pages of this book). *Woman's Home Companion* was a popular women's magazine. Its roots extended back to an 1874 Ohio publication called *The Home* which merged later with a children's monthly, the *Home Companion*. It carried short stories and topical articles of interest to women, often championing causes throughout the next several decades. By the 1950s, its focus was on home service and it had millions of readers, but mounting costs and competition caused a drop in revenue. The magazine ceased publication with the January 1957 issue.

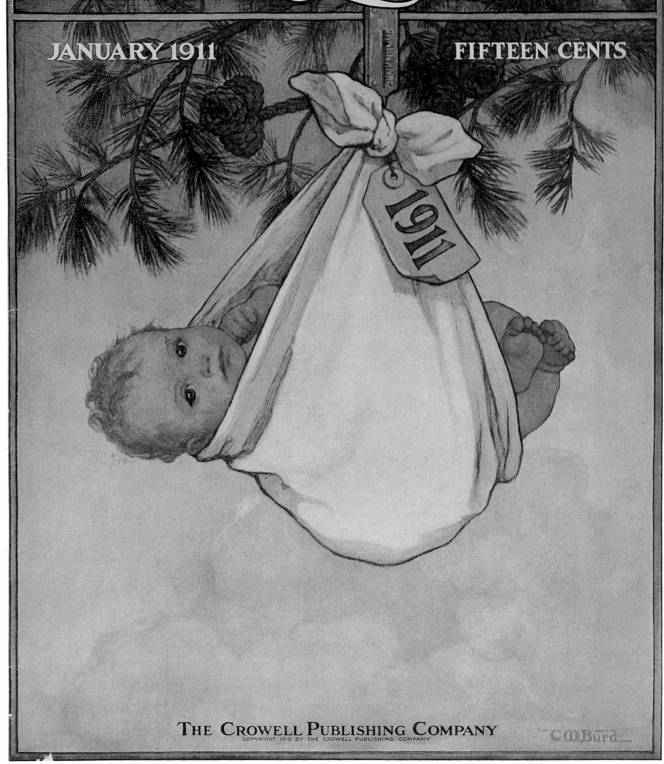

THE NEW YEAR'S
WOMAN'S HOME
COMPANION

JANUARY 1911   FIFTEEN CENTS

1911

THE CROWELL PUBLISHING COMPANY
COPYRIGHT 1910 BY THE CROWELL PUBLISHING COMPANY

95

ACKNOWLEDGMENTS

We would like to thank the people who
helped us in the creation of this book.

Brandt Aymar, senior editor at Crown Publishers, a division of Random House, for his continued enthusiasm and support; Jane Jordan Browne for representing us; and Susan B. Nicholson, for making her library and collection available to us, including items on pages 35, 58 (top left and bottom), 74, 84, 85, and 90.

In particular, we wish to thank two special friends, who, although they wish to remain anonymous, deserve recognition for their contribution to the success of this book. Thank you for so generously allowing us to photograph the beautiful items from your outstanding collection of antique advertising, seen on pages 16 (bottom), 19, 23, 25, 27, 33 (bottom), 34, 36, 38, 39, 40, 42 (bottom), 43, 44 (bottom), 45, 48–49, 53, 58 (top right), 59, 71, 73, 79, 83, 88, and 91.

Also, thanks to James Archie for letting us photograph the item on page 18, to Mrs. Anthony Guerriero for items on page 68, and Nancy and John Challenger for the sign on page 78.

All photography in this book is the work of Peter Basdeka, except photos taken by Andy Richmond on pages 18, 51, 66, 68 (bottom), 69, 74–75, and 95; Tom Fay, pages 68 (top) and 77; and Nabisco Brands, Inc., page 61.

The beautiful decorative borders and the illustration on page 2 were created by Clara M. Burd and appeared in "Baby's Record," published in 1913.

In addition, the following companies have granted permission for inclusion of items in this book: (Cover and 13) Courtesy of The William Carter Company. (3–4, 20 bottom, 64–65, 69) Reprinted by permission of Sterling Drug Inc. (5, 16–17) Permission to reproduce photos has been granted by The Mennen Company. (9) "Baby's Book"—Courtesy MetLife Insurance Co.; "Baby's Record"—Courtesy South Carolina National Bank. (10–11–12) Used with permission of Borden, Inc. (18–19) Courtesy of James Archie. (20 top) Mentholatum® is a registered trademark of the Menolatum Company. (21) Used with permission of Monticello

Drug Co. (22–23 left) Courtesy of SmithKline Beecham Consumer Brands. (23 right & 43 left) Rexall-Ft. Lauderdale, FL 33334. (24 bottom) Used by permission of Cadbury Beverages Inc. (25 right) © Avon Products, Inc. (26–28) Courtesy of Kellogg Company. (29, 61, 80–81) Courtesy of Nabisco Brands, Inc. (30–31) From archives of Coats & Clark Inc. Used by permission. (32, 87) Courtesy of Colgate-Palmolive Company. (42 top) Used with the permission of Pet Incorporated. (47) Used with permission, The Masterson Company, Inc. (48–49) "Munsingwear" is a registered trademark of Munsingwear, Inc. (54 bottom) Photo courtesy of Singer Sewing Company. (58 bottom) The registered KEWPIE trademarks and copyrights are used by permission of Jesco, Inc., Monrovia, California. (60) Reproduction authorized by Navistar International Transportation Corp. (63) Reproduced with the permission of A & F Pears Ltd. (67 top) Photo courtesy of SmithKline Beecham. (68) Used with permission of Mrs. Anthony Guerriero. (70 bottom) The J. Strickland Company owns and has exclusive use of the trademark, Hoyt's®. (72) © The Procter & Gamble Company. Used with permission. (76 bottom) Info compliments of Gulbransen, Incorporated. (77) SUNKIST is a registered trademark of Sunkist Growers, Inc., Sherman Oaks, California; ALPHABETICAL is a registered trademark of The Villa Park Orchard Association, Orange, California. (79) © Lucie Attwell Limited. (82) Warner-Lambert Company. (83) Compliments of Henry Heide, Inc., New Brunswick, New Jersey. (84) Reprinted by permission of Amoco Oil Company. (85) By permission of Capper Magazine, Stauffer Comm. Inc. (89) © Johnson & Johnson. (92) With permission of CSX Corporation, Richmond, Virginia. (93) From pages of *Ladies' Home Journal*.